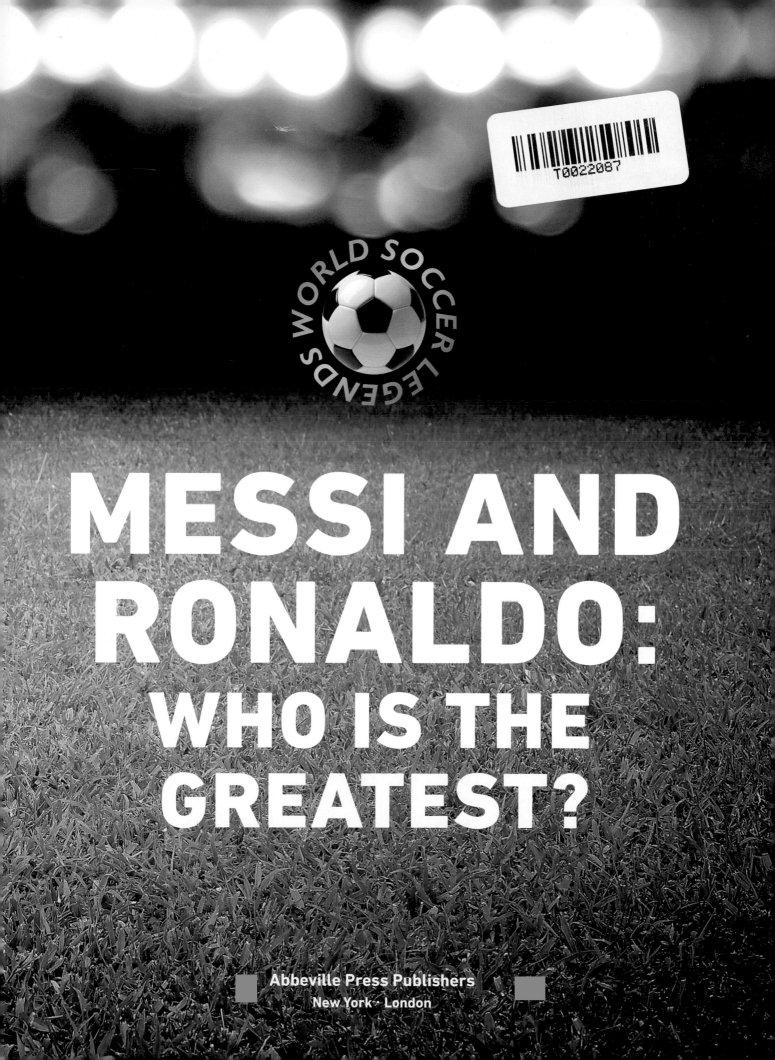

WORLD SOCCER LEGENDS

MESSI AND RONALDO:
WHO IS THE GREATEST?

Abbeville Press Publishers
New York · London

A portion of this book's proceeds are donated to the **Hugo Bustamante AYSO Playership Fund**, a national scholarship program to help ensure that no child misses the chance to play AYSO Soccer. Donations to the fund cover the cost of registration and a uniform for a child in need.

Statistics are current as of July 2020.

Text by Illugi Jökulsson
Design and layout: Árni Torfason

For the English-language edition
Project Editors: David Fabricant and Lauren Bucca
Copy Editor: Ashley Benning
Layout: Angela Taormina
Production Manager: Louise Kurtz

PHOTOGRAPHY CREDITS
Getty Images: p. 22 (Keystone), pp. 22–23 (Denis Doyle), pp. 24–25 (Shaun Botterill), p. 26 (Michael Steele), p. 27 (Jasper Juinen), pp. 30–31 (Christof Koepsel), p. 33 (Alexander Hassenstein-FIFA/FIFA), p. 34 (Shaun Botterill FIFA/FIFA), pp. 44–45 (Victor Carretero/Real Madrid), p. 52 right (David Ramos)

Shutterstock: front cover, Messi (Jose Breton-Pics Action), front cover, Ronaldo (Paolo Bona), pp. 2–3 (twobee), p. 6 and back cover, bottom (Marco Canoniero), p. 7 (Jose Breton-Pics Action), pp. 8–9 (Tomasz Czajkowski), pp. 10–11 (illpaxphotomatic), pp. 12–13 (Iakov Filimonov), p. 15 (ph.FAB), pp. 16–17 (Richard Cavalleri), p. 19 (ph. FAB), pp. 20–21 and back cover, top (ph.FAB), p. 28 (Natursports), p. 29 (Maxisport), pp. 32–33 (Marcos Mesa Sam Wordley), p. 35 (fstockfoto), p. 37 (Asatur Yesayants), p. 39 (AGIF), p. 41 (Ververidis Vasilis), p. 43 (ph.FAB), pp. 46–47 (ph.FAB), pp. 48–49 (Marcos Mesa Sam Wordley), p. 51 (Laszlo Szirtesi), p. 52 left (A.RICARDO), p. 53 top (Oleksandr Osipov), p. 53 bottom (MDI), pp. 54–55 (Jose Breton-Pics Action), p. 57 (istanbulphotos), pp. 58–59 (cristiano barni), p. 60 and back cover, center (Cosmin Iftode), p. 61 (Maxisport), p. 62 (Christian Bertrand), p. 63 (Cristiano Barni)

Wikipedia: p. 9 (U.S. Federal Government/Public Domain), p. 11 (U.S. Department of State/Public Domain), p. 12 (The Edge-Own work/Public Domain)

Please note: This book has not been authorized by Lionel Messi or Cristiano Ronaldo or persons affiliated with them.

This edition first published in the United States of America in 2020 by Abbeville Press, 655 Third Avenue, New York, NY 10017

First Edition
10 9 8 7 6 5

Library of Congress Cataloging-in-Publication Data

Names: Illugi Jökulsson, author.
Title: Messi and Ronaldo : who is the greatest? / Illugi Jökulsson.
Description: New York, NY : Abbeville Press Publishers, [2020] | Series:
   World soccer legends | Audience: Ages 7 and up | Audience: Grades 2–3 |
   Summary: "Compares two of the world's greatest soccer players, Messi
   and Ronaldo, with color photographs throughout" —Provided by
   publisher.
Identifiers: LCCN 2020032312 | ISBN 9780789213976 (hardback)
Subjects: LCSH: Messi, Lionel, 1987—Juvenile literature. | Ronaldo,
   1985—Juvenile literature. | Soccer
   players—Argentina—Biography—Juvenile literature. | Soccer
   players—Portugal—Biography—Juvenile literature.
Classification: LCC GV942.7.M398 I4515 2020 | DDC 796.334092/2 [B]—dc23
LC record available at https://lccn.loc.gov/2020032312

For bulk and premium sales and for text adoption procedures, write to Customer Service Manager, Abbeville Press, 655 Third Avenue, New York, NY 10017, or call 1-800-ARTBOOK.J4

Visit Abbeville Press online at www.abbeville.com.

CONTENTS

CRISTIANO RONALDO
WINGER/STRIKER
PORTUGAL

Christiano Ronaldo and Leo Messi have dominated world soccer for more than a decade. They rank with the greatest players in the history of the sport—and may be the greatest players of all time. This is their story.

THE WORLD'S

FULL NAME: CRISTIANO RONALDO DOS SANTOS AVEIRO
BORN: FEBRUARY 5, 1985
BIRTHPLACE: FUNCHAL, MADEIRA, PORTUGAL
HEIGHT: 6 FT 2 IN
CLUBS: SPORTING, MANCHESTER UNITED, REAL MADRID, JUVENTUS
CLUB GAMES: 841
CLUB GOALS: 629
INTERNATIONAL GAMES: 164
INTERNATIONAL GOALS: 99

LEO MESSI
WINGER/STRIKER
ARGENTINA

GREATEST

FULL NAME: LIONEL ANDRÉS
MESSI CUCCITTINI
BORN: JUNE 24, 1987
BIRTHPLACE: ROSARIO,
ARGENTINA
HEIGHT: 5 FT 7 IN
CLUB: BARCELONA
CLUB GAMES: 724
CLUB GOALS: 630
INTERNATIONAL GAMES: 138
INTERNATIONAL GOALS: 70

THEIR HOMETOWNS

RONALDO COMES FROM MADEIRA

This island in an archipelago of the same name lies 550 miles off mainland Portugal. It is 420 miles northwest of the coast of Morocco and 250 miles north of the Canary Islands, belonging to Spain.

Madeira, at 309 square miles, is about the size of New York City. The Portuguese started settling the island around AD 1420. Originally small-scale agriculture and fishing were the important industries, but in recent years, tourism has become increasingly significant. Madeira is home to around 290,000 people, similar to Orlando, Florida.

Cristiano Ronaldo is the youngest of four siblings. The eldest is Elma (b. 1973), then Hugo (b. 1975), and Katia (b. 1977). Their mother, Maria Dolores dos Santos Viveiros da Aveiro, worked as a cook, while their father, José Dinis Aveiro, was a gardener and utility man.

The family was troubled by the shadow of alcoholism. Though their father tried his best

PORTUGAL

Area: 35,600 square miles, similar to the states of Maine and Indiana
Population: 10.2 million, roughly comparable to North Carolina and Michigan
Capital: Lisbon, population approx. 500,000, similar to Sacramento, CA, and Atlanta, GA

to contain his addiction, he struggled badly. Soccer became Ronaldo's way of diverting his thoughts and escaping a sad situation. His talents soon became apparent, and from the outset, he trained with a burning ambition. To make sure that he never ended up in the same state as his father, he decided never to touch alcohol. He has kept his promise, except for the odd glass of champagne in special moments of triumph.

Ronaldo's mother was the true hero of his youth. She is a kind, loving woman and worked very hard to keep the family together. When people realized that her boy had serious talent, she made it possible for him to train and brought him to the attention of coaches. To this day, she supports her son in all his endeavors. Ronaldo's father proudly witnessed his son's breakthrough years at Manchester United but died in 2005, well before his time.

Cityscape of Funchal, Madeira, Portugal

THE PRESIDENT

Ronald Reagan was president of the United States when Maria and José had their last child. His first name, Cristiano, signifies his mother's deep Catholic faith. His father picked the second name and chose Ronaldo in honor of President Reagan. It was not so much Reagan's politics that drew José Dinis Aveiro's admiration—Reagan had simply been his favorite actor when he was growing up.

MESSI COMES FROM ROSARIO

This Argentinian city was established in the early 19th century, long after European settlers had driven all the indigenous population away. Rosario gradually became an important market town by the Paraná River. Agricultural products from the surrounding region were gathered here and transported to the capital city of Buenos Aires, 175 miles away.

The city grew rapidly in the 20th century. Now there are approximately 1.2 million people living in Rosario, comparable to Dallas, Texas, or San Jose, California.

Lionel Messi was born in Rosario on a Wednesday to a tightly knit and supportive family. He was the third son of Jorge Messi and Celia Cuccittini. Celia worked in a magnet factory, while Jorge was a manager in a steel factory. They had had two sons, Rodrigo (b. 1980) and Matías (b. 1982), before Lionel Andrés was born in 1987. Later, they welcomed the daughter Maria Sol (b. 1993). The family lived in a blue-collar neighborhood and didn't lack basic necessities, but they didn't possess much more than that.

Lionel, or Leo, was a shy and introverted boy who did not require much attention. Early on,

ARGENTINA

Area: 1 million square miles, a little less than one-fourth of the United States
Population: 50 million, roughly one-sixth of the U.S. population
Capital: Buenos Aires, metropolitan population 13.5 million, approximately equal to Los Angeles

Messi's Birth Date:
June 24, 1987
Wednesday
Zodiac sign: Cancer
Birthstone: Pearl
Birth flower: Rose

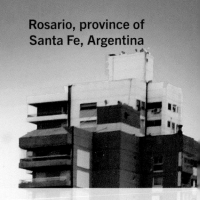

people noticed that he loved playing around with a soccer ball and could occupy himself with one for hours. His grandmother Celia often looked after him while his parents were working.

There is a family story that once when Granny Celia was taking care of Leo, she thought that he might enjoy playing with some older boys at a nearby soccer field. The coach was not impressed because Leo was very small and looked likely to start crying or get hurt when the big boys took the ball away from him. Still, the coach agreed that the boy could try, but he would have to leave if he started crying.

As soon as little Leo set foot on the field, he blossomed and showed astonishing skill. The coached watched openmouthed as little Leo accelerated past one bigger boy after another. This kid was clearly something special.

THE SINGER

Messi's parents were great fans of Lionel Ritchie, who was known for a string of hit songs in the 1980s, such as "Say You, Say Me," "Hello," and "All Night Long (All Night)." It is a sign of the couple's loving nature that they would name their third son after this singer of great love songs.

MESSI GROWING UP

Messi started playing for the Newell's Old Boys team in Rosario at a very young age. Everybody could see that he was ridiculously skillful with the ball and wasn't interested in anything but playing soccer. When he was around 10 years old, however, it became clear that he was not growing as he should. He had a growth hormone deficiency, and it looked like he would never be more than five feet tall. At that height it wouldn't matter how much skill and potential he had—he would never become a professional player. A treatment was available, but the Messis could not afford it. The major team River Plate of Buenos Aires planned to pay for the treatment in return for securing Messi for their team, but an economic crisis in Argentina made the club back away from this offer.

Messi's father then managed to get the major team Barcelona in Catalonia, Spain, to take a look at his son. When coach Carles Rexach saw the 11-year-old Messi demonstrate his skills and tricks, he immediately decided to sign the prodigy.

Finalizing the deal was delayed for a while, though, while the need to start Messi's hormone treatment became more pressing. His father then informed Barcelona that other clubs had also shown interest in Messi, one of them being Barça's rival Real Madrid. The negotiation was so urgent, then, that the first contract was signed on a napkin. In February 2001, the short and slight 14-year-old Messi moved to Barcelona. He started growing as soon as his treatments began, and the Barcelona directors could not wait to see this young genius start to make his mark at the club's famous home stadium, Camp Nou.

The Newell's Old Boys stadium has been in the Parque Independencia neighborhood of Rosario since 1911 and is commonly called El Coloso del Parque (the Colossus of the Park).

MORE THAN A SOCCER CLUB

It is an indication of Messi's levelheaded nature that he was not overawed upon arriving in Barcelona and visiting the world-famous home stadium Camp Nou in the Catalan city. Without missing a beat, the young boy joined the famous youth academy of Barça. The academy is known as La Masia, named after an old farm near Camp Nou that was its headquarters for many years.

For decades, Barcelona was in the shadow of Spain's most successful club, Real, in the capital of Madrid. But the loyalty and faith of the Barça fans have made the team legendary not only in Spain, but worldwide. In Spain, it is said that Barcelona is "more than a club."

Many world-renowned players have plied their trade with Barça. In the seventies, the Dutch genius Cruyff shone there and returned as the head coach of the so-called "Dream Team" in the late 1980s. It was Cruyff who insisted that Barcelona place greater emphasis on the youth coaching at La Masia and the one-touch passing style. Barcelona fully adopted this style, the main focus of which was to hold on to the ball and pass it around until an opportunity arose to break through the opposition defense. The reason why Leo Messi was a perfect fit with this "tiki-taka" style of Barça was that his game centered on holding on to the ball, running past defenders, and shooting unexpectedly.

Messi debuted for Barcelona when he came on as a substitute in the 82nd minute against city neighbor Espanyol on October 16, 2004. At the time, he was 17 years, 3 months, and 22 days old. He scored his first goal for the team on May 1, 2005, against Albacete. He instantly became an idol of Barcelona fans, and a vast number of soccer fans all over the world awaited further developments. Only a few years later, Messi had become the focal point of a great Barcelona team and was clearly on his way to become one of the best players in the world.

CAMP NOU

No stadium in the world has a more electric atmosphere than a packed Camp Nou. There is hardly ever an empty seat at the Barcelona home games, even with 99,354 places available. There are 12 independent nations in the world with fewer people than can be seated at Camp Nou.

A NEW MARADONA?

Early in Messi's career, he was often referred to as the new Maradona. Indeed, incredible skill and expressive joy are hallmarks of both players. Messi proved himself worthy of the moniker when he scored an unbelievable goal against Spanish team Getafe in April 2007, which bore an uncanny resemblance to a goal made by Maradona at the 1986 World Cup against England. Look these goals up on YouTube!

RONALDO'S HUNGRY HEART

Just as with Messi, for a time it seemed that a medical condition might destroy a young Cristiano Ronaldo's hopes of reaching the elite ranks. At home in Funchal, it became evident that he was far ahead of other boys his age, not just in terms of talent, but also in terms of ambition and concentration. At that time, he was also emotional and sometimes shed tears when his feelings got the better of him. But Ronaldo grew up to be big and strong, training with an almost violent intensity, and began to see the results when he was 12 years old. Sporting in Lisbon, one of the country's major soccer powers, brought Ronaldo to the Portuguese capital. It was tough for the boy to leave his hometown, but he was truly living the dream when he joined the Sporting youth academy. Two years later, he left school at his mother's urging to devote himself entirely to soccer. At that point, he thought that he might be able to turn semipro in the future and did not miss school.

"I was not dumb but I was not interested in school," he admitted in an interview later. "I was expelled after I threw a chair at the teacher. He disrespected me."

Respect has always meant a lot to Ronaldo, and he will not be put down by anybody. "I'm determined, I'm strong, very quick, and I'm very, very professional."

But when he was 15, Ronaldo's heart seemed to be playing tricks on him. He suffered from a so-called "racing heart," a form of tachycardia. His resting heart rate was faster than normal. Fortunately, modern medicine came to his aid, and a laser was used to cauterize the source of the problem. Ronaldo was operated on in the morning and came out of anesthesia at the end of the afternoon. He started training again a few days later.

Since then, only hunger has driven Ronaldo's heart—his hunger for success, victories, and an endless stream of goals.

VISIONARY?

When Cristiano Ronaldo was 14, he was certainly very promising for his age, but few entertained the idea that he could become one of the best and most famous players in the world. But he could look beyond Sporting's stadium. He told his practice partner that he would progress to Manchester United, and added: "And after a few years there, I'll go to Real Madrid."

TO MANCHESTER UNITED

On October 7, 2002, the 17-year-old Cristiano Ronaldo made his debut in the Portuguese Primeira Liga. Sporting's opponent on that day was Moreirense. Ronaldo wasted no time in showing what he could do, scoring two goals in a 3–0 victory for Sporting. With that, he had instantly played his way to a regular spot on the Sporting team. At the time, he played mostly on the right wing and did not score many goals. But his talent was plain to see, and in the summer of 2003, many major teams in England were eyeing him, including Liverpool and Arsenal. At this stage, however, Manchester United came to Lisbon to play a practice match with Sporting. Another reason for the match was to take a good look at the young Ronaldo. Sporting won the game and Ronaldo played superbly. The renowned Manchester United head coach, Sir Alex Ferguson, had been thinking about making an offer for the young player. The story goes that on the way to the airport the players urged Ferguson so hard to make the move and get Ronaldo that the United bus turned around, went back to meet with the Sporting directors, and secured Ronaldo's signature. Whether this is true or not, Ferguson is on record saying that the new recruit was one of the most exciting young players he had ever seen.

Manchester United is one of the most famous, richest, and successful soccer teams in the world, and at the time when Ronaldo transferred there, it was head and shoulders above all others. The club's home stadium, Old Trafford, holds 75,000 spectators, and to show what a favored destination it is to many soccer fans, it is called the Theater of Dreams. Although Ferguson was a huge fan of Ronaldo from the outset, he did not throw the Portuguese youngster in at the deep end, but gave him time to adapt. Gradually, it became apparent that Ronaldo was not just a quick and aggressive winger, but a leader on the field, with an extraordinary eye for goals and a shot to match the best. In the 2006–2007 season, he finally emerged as a goal scorer, with 23 goals in all competitions combined, won a number of personal honors, and became champion of England for the first time. But that was only the beginning.

ON THE SAME TEAM?

In the summer of 2003, Barcelona was one of the teams Ronaldo's agent contacted to offer his client's services. But the Catalan club was not overly interested and Ronaldo went to England. What would have happened if the Barça directors had been quick to think and had grabbed Ronaldo's signature? Messi was already making a name for himself at La Masia, but could the two have prospered on the same team? Would one of them have had to make way for the other? Or would they have struck up such a partnership that it would have made it futile for other teams even to show up against them?

May 27, 2009: Cristiano
Ronaldo in action during
the UEFA Champions
League final match between
Barcelona and Manchester
United at the Olympic
Stadium in Rome, Italy

May 27, 2009: Cristiano Ronaldo and Lionel Messi during the UEFA Champions League final match between Barcelona and Manchester United at the Olympic Stadium in Rome, Italy

THEIR FIRST ENCOUNTERS

Messi and Ronaldo first met on the soccer field during Barcelona and Manchester United's clash in the semifinals of the European Champions League in the 2007–2008 season. By then, both had taken center stage with their respective teams. Messi scored six goals leading up to the semifinals, Ronaldo seven. The first game was played at Camp Nou in Barcelona on April 23, 2008. United was awarded a penalty kick in the third minute, but Ronaldo fired past the goal. After that, Barcelona attacked for the majority of the game, but there were few chances and the match ended in a scoreless draw.

In the second game, Paul Scholes scored an early goal for United. Although Barça (as the club is most often called in Spain) attacked furiously, with a lively Messi at the front, Ronaldo and company held out and won the game. That meant that United had made it to the European Champions League final match, which was to be played in Moscow. In that game, United faced the London outfit Chelsea. Ronaldo scored early in the game, but Chelsea equalized and a penalty shootout was needed for a decisive result. Ronaldo failed to score from the penalty spot, but United won nevertheless. And so the Portuguese player had won the European Champions League for the first of five times!

THE ULTIMATE PRIZE

BALLON D'OR 2008: RONALDO I

The Ballon d'Or (French for the Golden Ball) is awarded at the end of each year by the magazine *France Football* to the most outstanding male player. The inaugural award was presented in 1956 to English winger Stanley Matthews.

Before 2008, only eight players had received the award more than once: Dutchmen Johan Cruyff and Marco van Basten earned it three times each. The Argentinian Alfredo Di Stéfano, Germans Franz Beckenbauer and Karl-Heinz Rummenigge, Englishman Kevin Keegan, Frenchman Michel Platini, and Brazilian Ronaldo Nazario took the prize twice each.

In 2007, the Brazilian player Kaká with Real Madrid received the honor. Cristiano Ronaldo placed second, while the 20-year-old Messi came in fourth.

After leading Manchester United to victory in the 2007–2008 Champions League and scoring 8 goals, and then scoring a stunning total of 42 goals in 49 games for United during the full season, Ronaldo won the Ballon d'Or at the end of 2008 by a wide margin. Messi came in second. At that point, he was not yet the goal machine he would later become, having "only" amassed 16 goals. But his importance for his Catalan team was growing fast.

Johan Cruyff was a leader in Ballon d'Or awards before the current rivalry, taking the prize in 1971, 1973, and 1974, and shown here playing for the Netherlands.

Fellow Portuguese player Eusébio presents Ronaldo of Manchester United his first Ballon d'Or during the UEFA Champions League Draw at the Grimaldi Center in Monte Carlo, Monaco, on August 28, 2008.

BALLON D'OR 2009: MESSI I

A year after Barcelona was eliminated by Man. United in the semifinals of the European Champions League, Messi and Barcelona got their chance to settle the score.

This time the two teams met in the final itself. Messi was in outstanding form under the coaching of the great Pep Guardiola and led his team not only to victory in Spain's top-tier La Liga, but swatted away all opposition in the European Champions League to make it to the final at the Olympic Stadium in Rome. The team had by then defeated France's Lyon, German giant Bayern Munich, and England's Chelsea in the knockout stage.

Meanwhile, Ronaldo was having a quiet start with the European Champions United. He didn't score until the Round of 16, when United eliminated Inter Milan. In the quarterfinals, he ensured a United victory over Porto of Portugal, and in the semifinals, United and Ronaldo were firing on all cylinders. He scored two goals in a victory over English rival Arsenal, and United got the opportunity to defend the European title.

The match was an anticlimax for the United fans. Barcelona controlled the match, and Messi played freely and expressively, while Ronaldo appeared shackled. First, Cameroonian forward Samuel Eto'o scored after outwitting the United defense, and late in the game, Messi ensured the win when he scored with a rare header from a crossfield pass by midfield maestro Xavi.

Messi scores the second goal for Barcelona during the UEFA Champions League final between Barcelona and Manchester United at the Olympic Stadium in Rome on May 27, 2009.

BALLON D'OR 2010: MESSI II

Although the Argentinian national team, with Messi leading the line, did not do all that well at the 2010 World Cup in South Africa, the star attacker still won the Ballon d'Or at the end of the year for the second time. The deciding factor was his stupendous showing in La Liga, where Barcelona was virtually unbeatable. Messi scored 47 goals in 53 games for the Catalan team, and in La Liga he scored 34 goals in 35 games!

During the same time, Ronaldo was doing exceptionally well in his first year with Real Madrid, scoring 33 goals in 35 games, but he had to watch Messi's teammates at Barça—the Spaniards Iniesta and Xavi—take the second and third slots for the Ballon d'Or. The duo had been instrumental in Spain becoming a world champion for the first time, employing their famous tiki-taka style of play (short passes, emphasis on possession) which they had learned at Barcelona.

Coach Pep Guardiola of Barcelona instructs Messi during the La Liga match between Barcelona and Real Madrid at Camp Nou in Barcelona on December 13, 2008.

GUARDIOLA

Barcelona's head coach at the time was the all-conquering Pep Guardiola, one of the most decorated managers in the world. It was Frank Rijkaard who first gave Messi an opportunity at Barça, but the player claims to have learned the most from Guardiola.

BALLON D'OR 2011: MESSI III

In 2011, Messi became the second player in history to win the Ballon d'Or three years running. Barcelona played exceptionally well and Messi piled the goals sky-high. After having scored both goals in a 2–0 win away at Real Madrid in the semifinals of the Champions League, the Argentinian and his teammates made short work of Manchester United in the final, in a matchup held in London. Messi scored a goal in an easy 3–1 victory and ended up top scorer in the European Champions League with 12 goals in 13 games.

In La Liga, Messi also scored constantly, totaling 53 goals in 55 games in all competitions. Barcelona defended the Spanish league title after a tough battle against Real. By now, it had become clear that Messi was no ordinary soccer player.

But Cristiano Ronaldo was also scoring a serious number of goals. He became La Liga's top scorer, playing in all 38 games and netting 46 goals! He was no less extraordinary than Messi.

The soccer world could hardly keep up with watching their goal-scoring exploits. Messi won the Ballon d'Or with a strong lead, while Ronaldo took second prize and Xavi third.

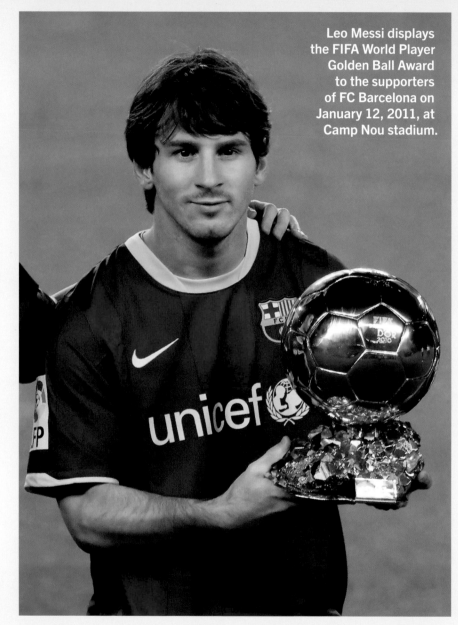

Leo Messi displays the FIFA World Player Golden Ball Award to the supporters of FC Barcelona on January 12, 2011, at Camp Nou stadium.

Messi watching the scoreboard during the match between FC Barcelona and RCD Espanyol at Camp Nou in Barcelona on May 8, 2011.

BALLON D'OR 2012: MESSI IV— MAKING HISTORY

Messi became the first player to win the Ballon d'Or four times, and he is still the only one to have taken the prize four times in a row. This was no easy feat. Messi scored no fewer than 73 goals in 60 games for Barcelona in the 2011–2012 season, unprecedented in Europe's strongest leagues. The previous record had belonged to the German Gerd Müller of Bayern Munich, who had scored 67 goals in the 1972–1973 season.

Messi constantly set new goal-scoring records, for example making five goals in a single game in the Round of 16 match against Bayer Leverku-

sen in the European Champions League. Unfortunately for Barça, the team lost in the semifinals against Chelsea, when Messi hit the crossbar from the penalty spot at the decisive moment.

Ronaldo also scored plenty, with enough goals to normally suffice for the Ballon d'Or: 60 goals in 55 games for Real Madrid. Again, he had to settle for second place, while Iniesta, Messi's teammate at Barcelona, was third. It was some consolation for Ronaldo that Real reclaimed the La Liga title from Barça, scooping an impressive 100 points from 38 games.

FIFA
BALLON
D'OR

March 29, 2013: Ronaldo in action in the rain during a La Liga match for Real Madrid at Santiago Bernabéu stadium in Madrid

BALLON D'OR 2013: RONALDO II

After Messi had won the Ballon d'Or for four years running and showed no sign of letting up, most of his rivals were probably losing their appetite for challenging him—not least those who were older players. But not Cristiano Ronaldo. He kept his nose to the grindstone and managed to wrestle the title from Messi in 2013.

Their performances were nearly identical. Messi did score more—60 goals in a total of 50 games, and Barcelona reclaimed the La Liga title—while Ronaldo scored 55 goals in 55 games. However, Ronaldo topped the Champions League scoring charts with 12 goals. Both of their teams were eliminated in the semifinals by German clubs, with Bayern Munich going on to beat Dortmund in the final.

The second place in the Ballon d'Or was claimed by Messi, and in third place was Bayern player named Franck Ribéry.

Cristiano Ronaldo with Nadine Angerer at the Kongresshaus on January 13, 2014, in Zurich, Switzerland

MESSI AND RONALDO
SHOW UP FOR THE WORLD CUP

Germany 2006: Italy beats France in a penalty shootout after an ill-tempered final. The 21-year-old Ronaldo and the 18-year-old Messi take part in the tournament for the first time. Ronaldo is an important player for Portugal. Messi plays fewer games, but does start one. Both players score one goal. Argentina is eliminated in the quarter-finals against Germany, but Portugal reaches fourth place after losing in the third-place decider, also against Germany.

South Africa 2010: In the first World Cup to be held in Africa, Spain wins gold for the first time after a 1–0 victory over the Netherlands. Portugal is eliminated by Spain in the Round of 16. Ronaldo is hardly noticeable and only scores one goal. Argentina, coached by Maradona, reaches the quarterfinals, where Germany delivers a rout. Messi—who is unstoppable in Barcelona colors during this period—struggles and doesn't score a single time in the tournament.

Brazil 2014: Messi drags a lackluster Argentinian team to the final, scoring four goals in the process, but Germany wins 1–0. (See p. 36.) Portugal fails to advance to the knockout stage, with Ronaldo scoring only one goal.

Russia 2018: Messi is far from his best and only scores one goal. Argentina is eliminated in the Round of 16 by a splendid French team, which goes on to win the tournament. Ronaldo gets off to a flying start with a hat trick against Spain and scores four goals in total. Nevertheless, Portugal fades and goes out in the Round of 16 against Uruguay.

Diego Maradona, head coach of Argentina, consoles Messi after the 2010 FIFA World Cup South Africa quarterfinal between Argentina and Germany at Green Point Stadium in Cape Town on July 3, 2010.

Portugal's Ronaldo in action against England during a World Cup Round of 16 match in Gelsenkirchen, Germany, on July 1, 2006

In the match between Portugal and England in the quarterfinals of the 2006 World Cup, Ronaldo is tackled by his Manchester United teammate Wayne Rooney, who is instantly sent off the field. Ronaldo's wink to his countrymen is taken as an indication that he exaggerated the seriousness of the challenge.

2014 WORLD CUP: MESSI'S LETDOWN

The 2014 World Cup in Brazil started well for Messi and Argentina. The team beat Bosnia 2–1 in the first match. Messi delivered a free kick that a defender then put in his own goal, and then he scored Argentina's second goal when he ran at the opposing defense and released a thunderous shot into the net. He then scored a magnificent goal in the final minute of the game against Iran, and Argentina won 1–0. In the last game of the group stage, Messi scored two goals off Nigeria, the second one with a great free kick, and Argentina won 3–2. Messi had by then scored four goals in three games.

In the Round of 16, Messi assisted on the game's only goal two minutes before the end of extra time in a very tough match against Switzerland. In the quarterfinal, Gonzalo Higuaín scored an early goal for Argentina against a classy Belgian team, which proved enough to win the game. In a demanding semifinal matchup against the Netherlands, Messi was obviously fatigued, the weight of Argentina looking to him to magically deliver chances and goals clearly

taking its toll. A dull match finally ended with an Argentinian triumph in a penalty shootout after even extra time had brought zero goals from regular play.

Still, this meant that Argentina had reached the final against Germany and had a chance to deliver World Cup gold to the Argentinian people a third time. This was Messi's chance to reach the same godlike status in the eyes of his compatriots as Maradona, who had won the 1986 World Cup to a large extent by himself. Unfortunately for Messi, this was not how things would turn out. He gave it everything he had, but he didn't show off his best qualities and didn't score, with the German substitute Mario Götze making the decisive goal in extra time. Head coach Joachim Löw had told Götze when he was heading out on the field: "Go out there and show that you can be as good as Messi."

For Messi, the result was a huge disappointment, and it was little consolation that at the end of the game he was declared the World Cup's Most Valuable Player.

Messi during the World Cup match between France and Argentina on June 30, 2018, in Kazan, Tatarstan, Russia

BALLON D'OR 2014: RONALDO III

Ronaldo's ridiculously impressive showing in the European Champions League brought him his third Ballon d'Or title in 2014. He broke the record by scoring 17 goals as Real Madrid steamrolled its way to an 11th European Champions League title. The crowning contribution was the Portuguese juggernaut scoring the tournament's final goal as Real quashed the challenge of its neighbor Atlético Madrid in the final in Lisbon. In total, Ronaldo scored 51 goals in 47 games, while Messi was relatively quiet compared to previous years and scored "only" 41 goals in 46 games.

Messi placed second in the Ballon d'Or running and third was Manuel Neuer, the captain of the German team which had taken World Cup glory from under Messi's nose in the final (see p. 36).

June 26, 2014: Ronaldo during the 2014 World Cup Group G game between Portugal and Ghana at Estádio Nacional Mané Garrincha in Brazil

BALLON D'OR 2015: MESSI V

Messi reclaimed the Ballon d'Or at the end of 2015, winning for a record fifth time! Barcelona was like a well-oiled machine, and Messi now had able deputies in the front line: the Uruguayan Luis Suárez and the Brazilian Neymar. This meant that Messi did not have to shoulder so much of the goal-scoring burden. Nevertheless, he was by far the top scorer, with 58 goals in 57 games in all competitions.

Although Barça, coached by Luis Enrique, won La Liga in the end, the team had to deal with a strong challenge from Real down to the wire, and Ronaldo took more goals than Messi: 61 in all.

It was the same story in the Champions League: the Barça machine worked flawlessly for the most part, and Messi thumped in the goals. In the semifinals, he played brilliantly against perennial German rivals Bayern Munich, scoring two wonderful goals at the end of the game, and earning Barcelona a place in the final. His old coach Pep Guardiola, now at Bayern, could only shake his head at his former protégé's genius.

In the other semifinal, Real lost to the Italian team Juventus. Ronaldo had pushed Real along with 10 goals, but could do no more. In the final, Barça dominated and won 3–1, but Messi went goalless in the game. The honor of top scorer was shared by three players: Messi, Ronaldo, and Neymar.

The same three players topped the Ballon d'Or vote, but here with Messi winning by a good margin, Ronaldo coming in second place, and Neymar placing third.

Messi during the UEFA Champions League game between Bayer 04 Leverkusen and Barcelona at BayArena stadium in Leverkusen, Germany, on December 9, 2015

MEETING ON THE FIELD

The biggest soccer teams in Spain, Real Madrid in the capital city and Barcelona in Catalonia, are two of the most famous and popular soccer clubs in the world. They meet at least twice every year—in La Liga, often in the Spanish Cup (Copa del Rey, the King's Cup), in the Supercopa, or even occasionally in the European Champions League. Games between these two teams are always passionately fought and closely followed. They are called "El Clásico" in Spain.

From 2009 to 2018, a new element of tension was added to the traditional battle between the Spanish giants in El Clásico: the rivalry between Ronaldo and Messi about who was the better player.

The dynamic duo had met three times in games between Manchester United and Barcelona (see p. 21), but now they entered a run of 30 games where they competed in the colors of Real and Barça.

On March 23, 2014, Messi scored the only hat trick ever in El Clásico games featuring the two star players. The match took place at the Real home stadium, the famous Santiago Bernabéu. Messi started by assisting a goal by Iniesta and then took a shot from a good position that went wide. This was French striker Karim Benzema's cue to equalize for Real and proceed to put his team in the lead with another goal.

Messi evened the score when he broke through the Real defense, but Ronaldo reestablished Real's lead after a dubious penalty. Next, Neymar was brought down inside the Real penalty box while receiving a pass from Messi, and Real defender Sergio Ramos was sent off. Messi scored from the penalty spot to equalize. At the very end of the game, Iniesta was flattened inside the penalty area and Messi scored again, bringing a nail-biting victory in a classic among Clásicos.

However, after this game, Messi went without a goal in El Clásico for three years, until two brilliant shots in a 3–2 win for Barça at Santiago Bernabéu in April 2017.

FAMOUS CLÁSICOS!

On October 7, 2012, Messi and Ronaldo were both at their best at Camp Nou in Barcelona. Ronaldo scored with a well-placed shot from the penalty area in the 22nd minute, but this was equalized with a well-balanced shot seven minutes later. Messi then scored with a fabulous free kick in the middle of the second half, but a few minutes later, Ronaldo evened things up after receiving a stunning assist from Mesut Özil. So the game ended 2–2 Barcelona–Real, 2–2 Messi–Ronaldo.

Cristiano Ronaldo and Lionel Messi in action during the UEFA Champions League final match at the Olympic Stadium in Rome, Italy, on May 27, 2009

TWO INTERNATIONAL GAMES

Messi and Ronaldo have met twice when representing their countries, both times at friendly training games.

The earlier game was played in Geneva, Switzerland, in February in the magical year 2011.

Ángel Di María scored the game's first goal for Argentina after a magnificent run and pass from Messi. Ronaldo equalized with a trademark powerful tap-in. Argentina then kept the upper hand and Messi eclipsed Ronaldo, but the winning goal only arrived in the final minute when Messi scored from the penalty spot.

The second game was played at Old Trafford in Manchester, England, in November 2014. It ended with a 1–0 Portugal win, but Guerreiro's winning goal only arrived late in the game after Messi and Ronaldo had both been replaced by substitutes at halftime.

Cristiano Ronaldo of Real Madrid and Lionel Messi of Barcelona in action at Estadio Santiago Bernabéu in Madrid on April 16, 2011, for La Liga

A MEMORABLE YEAR

Messi and Ronaldo met eight times in 2011. The first was a game between Argentina and Portugal in February, but an amazing round of games began in April, in which Real and Barcelona met 4 times in 17 days. First there was a La Liga game which ended 1–1. Messi and Ronaldo both scored on penalties. The final of the Copa del Rey came next. In a rather combative and dour game, Ronaldo finally broke the deadlock with a goal-scoring header in extra time.

A week later, the first of the two semifinals of the European Champions League was played on Real's home ground. In a very tough match, Messi pushed through and scored twice. The second was particularly special, with Messi weaving through almost all of Real's defense by himself. In the return game at Camp Nou, Barça attacked relentlessly, but the end result was a 1–1 draw in which neither Messi nor Ronaldo managed to score.

For the 30 games between Barcelona and Real Madrid featuring Messi and Ronaldo in La Liga, Copa del Rey, Spanish Supercopa, and Champions League:

BARCELONA WINS	14
REAL MADRID WINS	8
DRAWS	8
MESSI GOALS	20
RONALDO GOALS	18

UEFA EURO FINAL 2016: RONALDO TURNS THE TIDE

Portugal's road to the final for Euro 2016 was not particularly impressive. In the first match, the team could only pull off a 1–1 draw with Iceland (the national team comes from a tiny island of 330,000 people), and Ronaldo was clearly annoyed with the result. The next game brought a 0–0 draw with Austria, and in the third game, Portugal found itself trailing twice to Hungary. A loss would have meant that Portugal was out of the tournament. But Ronaldo finally kicked into gear, scoring two goals to bring Portugal a third draw and obtain a place in the knockout phase.

In the Round of 16, Portugal needed 117 minutes of extra time to score a single goal against Croatia to make it to the quarterfinals. Another grueling match followed, this time facing Poland, but Portugal emerged from a penalty shootout with a win. In the semifinals against Wales,

Ronaldo lifts the European Championship trophy for Portugal at the UEFA Euro 2016 Final at the Stade de France, Saint-Denis.

Ronaldo finally shone again, scoring on a well-placed header in the 50th minute. Soon after, he teed up Nani for another goal. Despite rather ponderous play, Portugal had reached the final against France.

France had played well and was a heavy favorite for the gold on its home turf, not least after Ronaldo went off injured in the 25th minute. He was clearly devastated when he was carried off the field. Against all odds, Portugal resisted the constant barrage from the French, and in the later stages of the game, Ronaldo showed up on the substitutes' bench and screamed encouragement to his teammates. In the final minutes of extra time, the substitute attacker Éder scored the game's only goal for Portugal, and Ronaldo and his crew celebrated a moment of glory that had been a long time coming.

January 17, 2016: Ronaldo in action during a La Liga match with Sporting Guon at Santiago Bernabeu stadium in Madrid, Spain

BALLON D'OR 2016: RONALDO IV

Ronaldo had no intention of backing off in the battle with Messi for the Ballon d'Or and ended up winning for the fourth time in 2016. The Portuguese forward's commanding performances in the Champions League were the main factor in the writers at *France Football* picking him over the Argentinian. In six games at the group stage, Ronaldo scored 11 goals, and at the knockout stage he added five more, making Real unstoppable. Only in the final match, facing city rivals Atlético Madrid, did Real have to settle for a draw in regular and extra time, but ground out a victory in the penalty shootout with Ronaldo scoring the winning shot.

Barcelona was quiet in the Champions League and lost in the quarterfinals to Atlético.

La Liga featured a hard battle for the top spot, but Barça won that competition in the end. For the first time since 2009, the league's top scorer was neither Messi nor Ronaldo; the Golden Boot went to Suárez, Messi's teammate at Barça.

Since Messi had been keeping a relatively low profile during the season, it was clear Ronaldo would claim the Ballon d'Or, holding all the aces of Portugal's Euro 2016 success and his own 13 goals in 13 international games for the year. Messi followed in second, and Atlético forward Antoine Griezmann was third.

BALLON D'OR 2017: RONALDO V

Messi didn't tell anyone at the time, but he later revealed that he had been a little hurt when he missed taking the Ballon d'Or at the end of 2017. Barcelona had admittedly lagged well behind Real both in La Liga and the Champions League, but Messi was far and away the top scorer in La Liga and had 10 goals at the group stage of the Champions League knockout phase, taking an ever larger creative and driving role in Barça's attack.

In contrast, Ronaldo only really hit top gear at the Champions League and scored 11 goals in the last five games, including three hat tricks and two goals in the final match where Real defeated Juventus 4–1.

So Ronaldo made things even in the eternal struggle with Messi for the Ballon d'Or, and at this point a decade had passed since anyone other than those two had received the prize. Ronaldo had by now taken on a pure striker's role, scoring many goals by attacking the ball within the penalty box but rarely taking defenders on and making runs from midfield. However, he was still fully capable of such bursts of acceleration.

Messi was second, and Neymar, who was now playing at French club Paris Saint-Germain, was third.

September 3, 2017: Ronaldo listens to the anthems prior to Hungary versus Portugal FIFA 2018 World Cup Qualifier match at Groupama Arena in Budapest, Hungary.

FAMILY AND CHILDREN

For a long time, the love lives of Ronaldo and Messi were taken as one example of their different characters.

When Messi was about to turn 20, he went back home to Rosario for Christmas break. While he was in Rosario, he ran into a woman named Antonella Roccuzzo. Messi had first met Antonella, a cousin of his childhood friend, when he was only five years old. They soon fell in love. They now live a happy, and very private, family life with their three sons: Thiago (b. 2012), Mateo (b. 2015), and Ciro (b. 2018). Lionel and Antonella were married in Rosario in 2017 and still have a tight bond with their home city.

Ronaldo took a longer time to settle down. He had a taste for partying and nightclubs, often accompanied by beautiful women. In 2010, the unexpected news broke that he had fathered a child with an unnamed woman and that he had sole custody of the boy, also named Cristiano. For a few years, Ronaldo was in a relationship with the Russian model Irina Shayk. In 2017 he surprised everyone with newborn twins, named Eva Maria and Mateo Ronaldo, who were carried by a surrogate. A few months later, Ronaldo's daughter Alana Martina was born to his fiancée, the Spanish model Georgina Rodriguez.

It will be interesting to see whether any of Messi's or Ronaldo's kids inherit their father's soccer ability!

Antonella Roccuzzo and Mateo watch Messi play at the Copa America Semifinals in the Mineirão, Belo Horizonte, Brazil, July 2, 2019.

June 3, 2017: Cristiano Ronaldo of Real Madrid, girlfriend Georgina Rodriguez and son, Cristiano Ronaldo Jr., at Juventus vs. Real Madrid, UEFA Champions League Final, National Stadium of Wales, Cardiff.

Above: Ronaldo and family celebrating with the UEFA Champions League trophy following his team's victory in the UEFA Champions League final between Real Madrid and Liverpool in 2018. Below: Neymar with his son David Lucca and teammate Messi with his son Thiago pose for a photo prior to a game, September 24, 2013, at the Olympic Stadium in Barcelona, Spain.

BALLON D'OR 2019: MESSI VI

Some thought Messi would retreat into his shell following the disappointment of the Ballon d'Or vote in 2018, when Croatian midfielder Luka Modrić claimed the prize and Messi didn't even make the top three. They turned out to be spectacularly wrong. Admittedly, in 2018–2019 Barcelona was not the same winning machine it had been in the days of Pep Guardiola and Luis Enrique, suffering a few glitches. However, Messi played his role of leader to perfection and was still the prime mover as his team convincingly claimed the La Liga title. Real Madrid had not come close to recovering after losing Ronaldo to Juventus.

But their failure to win the European Champions League was a huge disappointment to Messi and his teammates. After an emphatic 3–0 win over a sprightly Liverpool in the first game of the semifinals, most people had expected Barcelona to make its first final match appearance in four years. However, the English team conjured an amazing comeback at its home stadium and won 4–0.

In the final, Liverpool then beat fellow English team Tottenham. Messi readily admitted that it had been painful to watch Liverpool celebrating their victory.

Perhaps it was some consolation to Messi that he did end up as the top scorer in the Champions League and also had the better of Liverpool's representative for the Ballon d'Or, very narrowly emerging ahead of Dutch defender Virgil van Dijk. Ronaldo was a distant third. Ronaldo did not find it as easy to score in the defensive Serie A in Italy as he had in La Liga, but still did an outstanding job. It was a disappointment to him, and to Juventus, to be eliminated in the quarterfinals of the European Champions League by a young and exciting Ajax out of the Netherlands.

A FUNNY KID

Messi's middle son, Mateo, is a funny kid who likes to tease his dad. When Messi had recovered from the loss to Liverpool at Anfield, he revealed that Mateo had insisted on always being Liverpool when he was playing soccer with his dad and his big brother Thiago.

Lionel Messi during the UEFA Champions League Round of 16 match between Barcelona and Olympique Lyonnais at Camp Nou on March 13, 2019, in Barcelona, Spain

MILLIONAIRES

Messi and Ronaldo have become very rich from their soccer genius. It is no simple matter to evaluate their exact wealth, since a sizable portion of their income is from all sorts of sponsorship deals and endorsements, where the amounts are not always publicly available. However, it is clear that the two are among the richest athletes in history and the only soccer players on the level of the biggest NBA stars, boxers, golfers, and tennis pros.

In 2019, *Forbes* calculated which athletes had made the most money in the previous 10 years.

The top five list shows the two soccer stars holding their own in an elite group:

1. Floyd Mayweather, boxing, $915 million
2. Cristiano Ronaldo, soccer, $800 million
3. Lionel Messi, soccer, $750 million
4. LeBron James, basketball, $680 million
5. Roger Federer, tennis, $640 million

Both Messi and Ronaldo have been penalized in Spain for not having declared all their income correctly to the tax authorities. Messi's case centered on a sum of approximately 4 million dollars, but for Ronaldo it was 14 million dollars. Both claimed that the people who handled their finances had made mistakes and they themselves hadn't known anything about it.

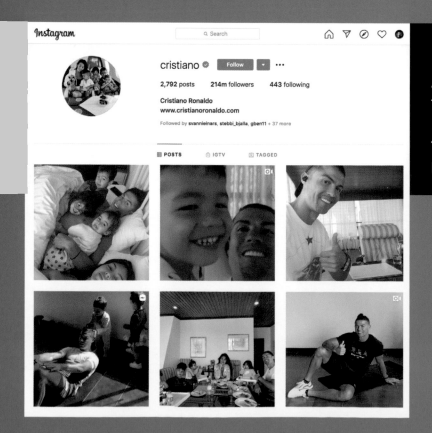

INSTAGRAM HEROES
As of April 2020, Ronaldo is the most followed person on Instagram with 214 million followers. Messi is in eighth place with 148 million.

ADVERTISING KINGS

Any marketing executive would be thrilled to get Messi and Ronaldo to advertise their clients' products! Currently, Messi has marketing deals with Pepsi, Adidas, Dolce & Gabbana, and is the global brand ambassador of Tata Motors, while Ronaldo has sponsorship deals with Tag Heuer, Clear Haircare, and Nike—and the list doesn't end there for either star.

SURPRISE

In the summer of 2018, Ronaldo surprised most people when he decided to leave Real Madrid for Italian champion Juventus. His stated aim was to take on a new environment and a new challenge. Later, he added that he had not been feeling supported enough by Real Madrid's president Florentino Pérez.

At Juventus, Ronaldo hit the ground running. As he explained:

"The first thing I do [when I get to a new club] is be myself and nothing more. My work ethic is always the same. If a business owner arrives and starts to crack down on everyone, people will not see him as a leader. They will say, 'This is my boss, but he does not treat me well.'"

"You must be humble, learn that you don't know everything. If you're smart, you get little things that make you better as an athlete. At Juve I adapted perfectly. They saw that there's nothing false about me. 'He is Cristiano, and he is what he is because he takes care of himself.' It is one thing to speak and another to do. Why [else] did I win five Ballon d'Ors and five Champions Leagues?"

Ronaldo leads Juventus in a 2–0 win over Lazio at the Serie A in Turin, Italy, on August 25, 2018.

NO SURPRISE

For many years, people have speculated whether Messi might leave Barcelona and try his luck with another major team. Some people have a very hard time picturing him in any other shirt than the "blaugrana" (blue and red) of Barcelona, and he hasn't indicated that he ever considered leaving for professional reasons. However, he revealed a few years ago that, in 2013, he had been very close to leaving Spain because he felt that the tax authorities were treating him unreasonably. After that dispute was settled, he has not mentioned the possibility again. However, before the coronavirus curtailed the 2019–2020 season, it had become clear that Messi was no longer completely content at Barça. He led a sort of player revolt against the board administrators and did not hide his part in these actions. But it would still clearly be a huge step for such a loyal soccer player as Messi to leave the club.

Besides, only a select few world-class teams could afford him. So don't expect any surprises!

WILL THEY BECOME THE COACHES?

RONALDO:
"My future as a coach?
I don't rule it out."

MESSI:
"I haven't thought about it. I don't want to [think about it]. Everyone lives in their own way—I try to go year after year, calmly. When the day arrives, we will see. I will find the path to follow, I will grab hold of it and we will see how everything goes. [. . .] Right now, I don't see myself as a manager. You never know what will happen, though. I heard Zidane once say he would never be a manager and then he ended up going into it. I don't see myself coaching but I don't know what will happen."

October 22, 2016: Messi celebrates a goal at the La Liga match between FC Barcelona and Valencia CF in Valencia, Spain.